Simple is Deep

SHARAM

EDITED BY
Shahed & Nafiseh

TALIA

SIMPLE IS DEEP
SHARAM

Edited by: Shahed & Nafiseh
Paperback 1st Edition
Published in 2023 by:

TALIA

Talia, Friends of Existence, Inc.
Website: www.taliafriends.org
Email: talia@taliafriends.org

Copyright © 2023 by Talia, Friends of Existence, Inc.
ISBN 978-0-9600047-5-1

All rights reserved.

No part of this book may be reproduced, stored in a retrieval system, or transmitted in any form or by any means, electronic, mechanical, photocopying, recording or otherwise, without the prior written permission of the publisher.

Many thanks to Melina H and Chris Pearson for their invaluable help.
Cover Art & Paintings: Sharam
Page Layout & Book Design: No Mind Design

MORE BOOKS
by Sharam

ORDER NOW ON:
Sharam.org

Gentleness Works

A Monk's View of Life

Clarity for Your Day

Don't Beat Yourself Up

You Are Your Happiness

The Book of Existence
Part One

Mysticism
The Psychology of Love

Happiness
The Essence of Your Being

Decoding Love
Understanding is Compassion

From Negativity to Joy

The Power of Let-Go

Happiness
The Name of Our Soul

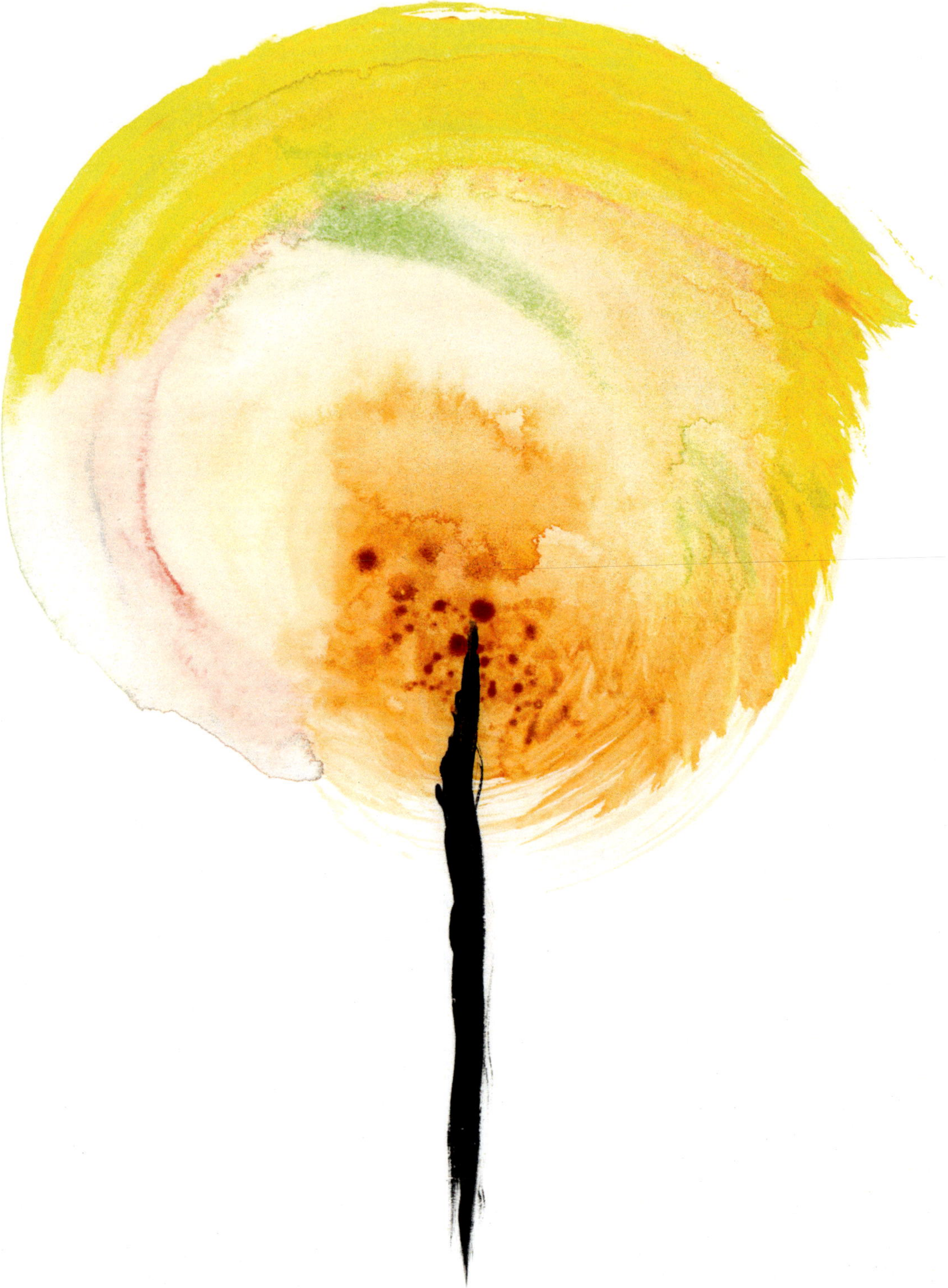

INTRODUCTION

Imagine one hand that is connected to a super-advanced brain. Now imagine that this hand has eight billion fingers. We are the same. Human souls are the eight billion fingers of a highly advanced energy. When humans go deeper than their mind, they reach their soul. This soul is connected to this highly intelligent source. We call this source the truth. Often, when we get to our depth, we see that everything is so simple. The truth is simple. The truth is deep. So simple is deep.

    My life was very hard, and nothing was working. Things would fall apart all the time. Then many, many years passed, and I noticed things were not falling apart as much because my life was becoming more simple. As I understood things in a simple way, I was also becoming happier. Things were becoming exciting and fun. So when there is simplicity, life works. The mind is complicated, it is convoluted and superficial. This superficiality causes problems in life. It makes life hard. Once I realized the beauty of simplicity and the importance of living from my depth, life became pure joy. Simplicity is so worth it.

— Sharam

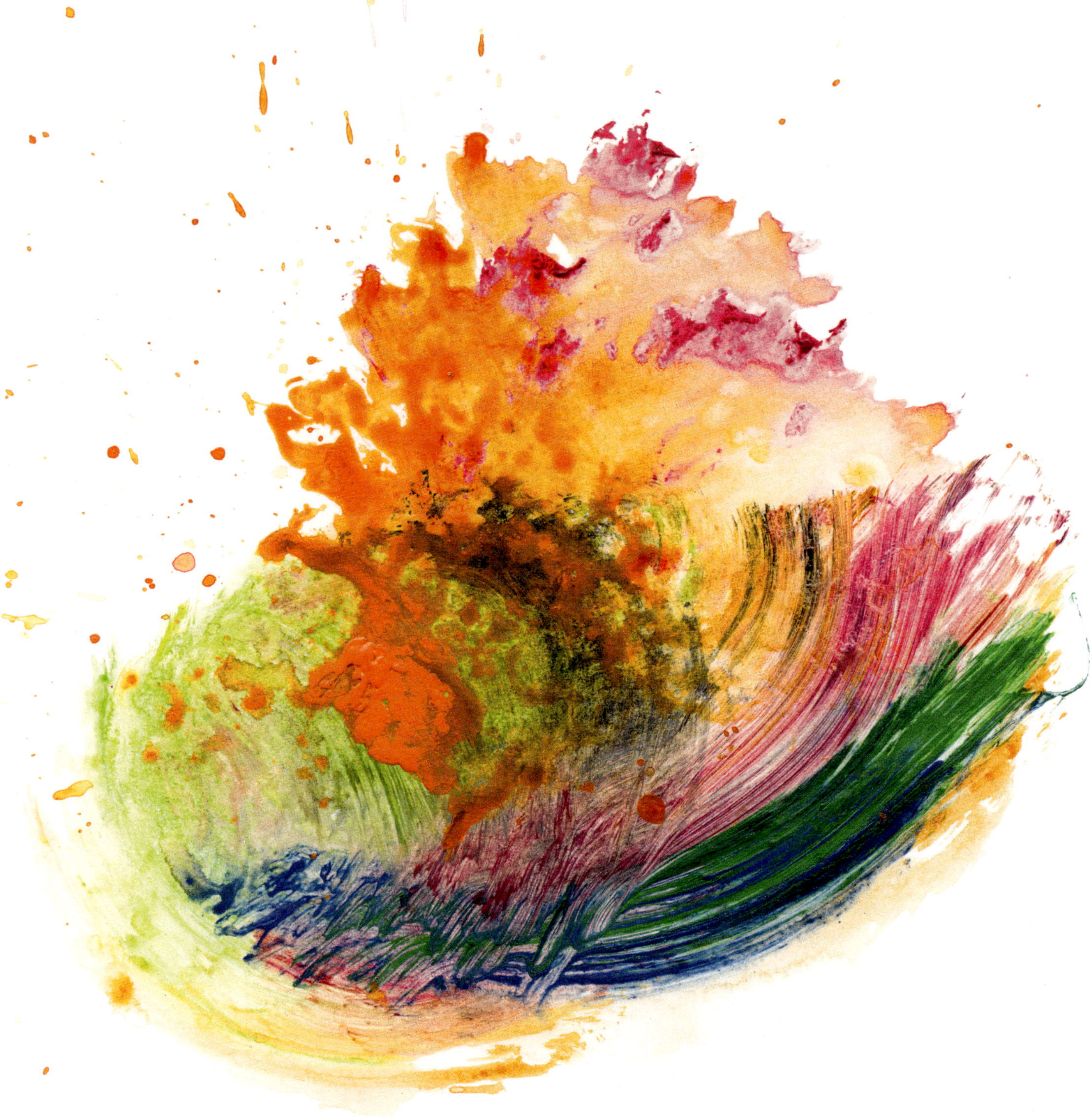

When we are totally ourselves, we become free and our lives work. We are taught by society not to be ourselves. We are told to worry about other people's judgments. At times, as children and adults, we are labeled stupid and not good enough. Society is very cruel. From childhood, our innocence is taken away from us through negative labels, and that is why we lose our essence, the essence that has been given to us by God. Our real self is what makes us happy and successful. It gives us a beautiful life. But because of society, we are forced away from this inner essence, and instead, we live with a fake and lower quality version of ourselves. The loss of our essence causes us to operate from the lower chakras and get stuck there, sometimes for the rest of our lives. We become stuck with worrying, negative feelings, and wanting to control everything in our lives. These are all signs that show we have gone astray.

     Mysticism is an effort to lead us back to our inner essence. Mysticism says there should be no goal, but if we are stuck in the lower chakras, a goal will help us to see and work on our issues and limitations and not get discouraged. When we advance, we rediscover our essence. Then we won't need goals. We will feel free all the time. Before we find our real selves, life is full of worry and problems, but once we find our real selves, we become one with Existence. We become enlightened. Society has given us a goal, and that is to make money and become rich. But our spiritual goal is to get to the point where we do not need goals, to get back to our real essence, to our inner freedom.

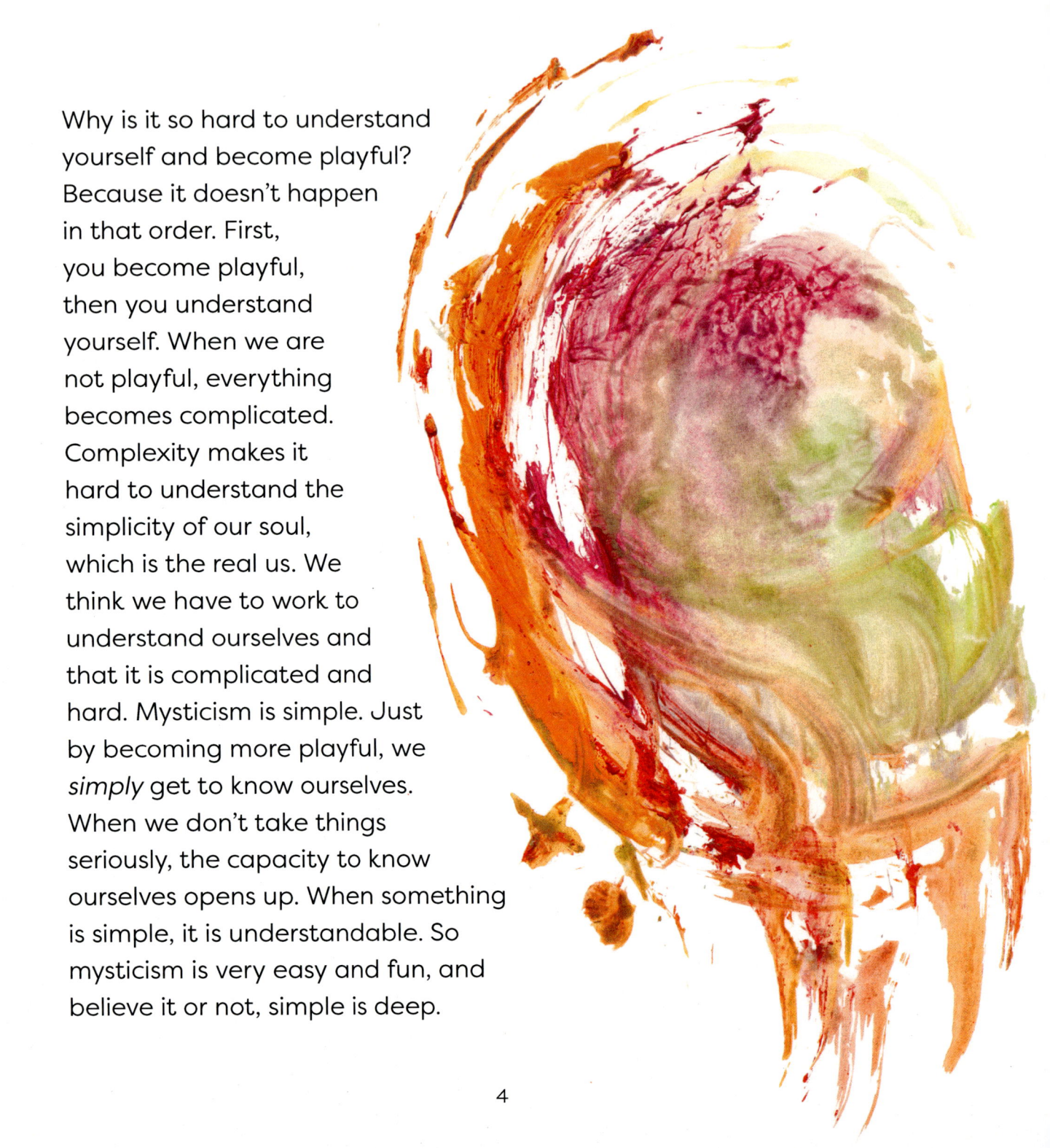

Why is it so hard to understand yourself and become playful? Because it doesn't happen in that order. First, you become playful, then you understand yourself. When we are not playful, everything becomes complicated. Complexity makes it hard to understand the simplicity of our soul, which is the real us. We think we have to work to understand ourselves and that it is complicated and hard. Mysticism is simple. Just by becoming more playful, we *simply* get to know ourselves. When we don't take things seriously, the capacity to know ourselves opens up. When something is simple, it is understandable. So mysticism is very easy and fun, and believe it or not, simple is deep.

The ego is there for us to pay attention to it. Existence has given us the ego, so we can witness it. Witnessing the mind and how we think is the best way for us to become aware. By witnessing, we learn the ways of the ego. Then every time the ego comes up, we pay attention to it and our awareness grows. This is our homework as a mystic or someone who wants to get to know the deeper part of themselves. This is easier when we are playful because we can look without judgment. A lot of people are playful, but they are not mystics. That playfulness is good, but it doesn't get them far. If you are a mystic and you are playful, you can pay attention and see yourself and your negativities much easier.

There are two different kinds of understanding. One is with our mind, which happens, for example, when we learn new things. The second happens when we hear a truth from our soul. With this second type of understanding, we are expanding our consciousness. Our consciousness becomes vaster. Our soul is sleeping, but when we hear the truth of Existence, we come to the moment, and the moment expands our soul. Actually, it expands our awareness of the soul. This truth really comes from our own soul. Our soul is one with Existence. It is as if our soul opens a door to a part of itself that we were not aware of. Our soul contains all the truth of Existence, but we have to become aware to be able to access all that inner knowledge. Deeper understanding is the way we access a new part of our consciousness. Everyday learning, that which comes from the mind, can make us heavy, but deep understanding makes us as light as a feather. Our consciousness expands, and we fly. We feel so much freedom.

Our mind can
be a bridge to
our soul with deep
understanding,
or it can become a
hindrance to the soul
with anger, jealousy,
worrying, or with
the ego in general.
Sometimes, when
we understand
deeply, we
might not even
remember it
as a piece of
information. The
mind steps aside
and the truth comes
out of our soul. The
mind might come in later
to remember it, but the
expansion of the soul has
already happened.

Using the mind only for maintaining our ego and looking good in the eyes of others is the wrong use of the mind. The mind has been given to us to be in the service of our soul. Our soul isn't concerned with politics, how chemistry works, geography, or history. These are all man made. They have nothing to do with the soul. Focusing on these should not be the only business of the mind. Understanding the layers of our soul is the right use of the mind. When we understand, we let go and the heart opens. The energy of the soul comes through the heart and heals the layers of the soul. Understanding breaks the prison that we call ego. Then we feel more alive, which means we come to the moment, and experience is pure happiness.

The mind is usually in conflict with our soul. For example, we set a goal to do something. We do it for two or three days, and then it becomes hard and we stop. Because we quit, the mind condemns us, and we feel bad. But it is possible that what the mind wants us to do is not what our soul really needs, so we just don't feel like doing it. It becomes hard for us to do that task if the soul isn't in agreement. It is actually very good that we don't want to do something that is hard for us. It's better we do something that is easy for us and do it wholeheartedly and with totality. In this way, we will be successful. We see that conflict between the mind and soul happens because the mind is the agent of society and wants to impose things on us that don't suit us. This keeps us in conflict. When our understanding deepens, we give space for our soul to operate. We become happy. This is letting go. This is allowing and accepting. So having a goal is okay, but ultimately, we need to go beyond goals.

The soul goes with the laws of
freedom. The body goes with
the laws of bondage. It is limited
by the pressure of gravity, which
makes it heavy. The soul flies into
the sky, while the body is pulled
down to earth. The soul is so light
and is everywhere.

Sometimes, Existence works with us, and we don't even know it. This is important because the mind can interfere with and hinder our growth. That is why Existence works in subtle ways with a person who is committed to working on themselves, so the mind will not catch on. We might think we are not working on ourselves, but that is not the case.

All thinking comes from society. It has nothing to do with our soul. Society demands that we obey its ways, but most of its ways are destructive and have very little to do with love. They are mostly ego-based. So what others think of us doesn't have much value, because their judgments are mostly based on society's thinking, and society doesn't have a soul. It is all about ego.

Success means, in the view of many, we have become important. It means that in the eyes of society, we are not only accepted, but also seen as distinguished and outstanding. Society is all about competition. This creates ego and pulls us down. People get destroyed by success because they become more deeply involved with or identified with society. They become slaves to it. Our desire for success is never ending. As we want to be more and more successful, we lose contact with our higher self, which is softness and love. The ideal is to have both success and softness, but when the ego gets involved, we think we are the most important person. All of a sudden, other people become less valuable to us because we think we are better than they are. We have separated ourselves from others, and any separation creates misery. Why? Because subconsciously, we start treating people in a subhuman way. Then people start disliking us. But if our awareness and consciousness are expanded, this separation won't happen. So if you find yourself successful, make sure to expand your consciousness at the same time. Meditate, and watch and understand your behavior and what is inside of your unconscious more deeply.

In this day and age, the mind has been developed. That is why we have riches, technology, and influence. Most people spend the majority of their time in the mind. It is very rare to find someone who comes from the heart because the mind dominates in society. Being courteous today is mostly used as an asset in the business world. It is basically a commodity or a sales technique. If you are nice, you are more successful. So society looks at niceness as an object. Coming from the heart is very different, and it's very rare to find a mind that can work with or meet with the heart. When we become more spiritually advanced, we have both—the heart and the mind functioning beautifully together. The heart is a door to the soul, and the soul is pure oneness or pure love. As mystics, we go beyond unconscious love—love that is from the mind or from our conditionings—and move into the purity of the soul.

Love is rooted in our soul, not just in the body. The body is part of the soul. It is the more condensed part of the soul. The essence of love comes from our soul.

Why do we push people away? Because we don't know what love is. Somebody might come to us with love, but because we don't recognize it, we might think, they want something from me. For example, my daughter wants a cookie, that's why she is being nice to me, or she wants to get away with something. We might even have all these thoughts unconsciously. It boils down to not recognizing love. But when we have love, we recognize love, and we never push it away. So if someone pushes you away when you are loving, it is just because they don't know love. That is all. It is so simple. We hurt people by not accepting their love, and we hurt ourselves because we are not aware. We do things without knowing we are doing them, and we miss out on love.

There are three stages in life. The first stage is when we don't know what love is, and because of this, we are miserable. Next, we love, but it is conditional. If people love me, I love them, and I am happy. If they don't, I am miserable. Our happiness depends on others; therefore, it is conditional. Then we move one step higher to unconditional love. With unconditional love, we are always happy and always blissful. Our love is a state of being and isn't dependent on others. When we are blissful, we get lots of blessings. For example, if there is a problem in our life and things become hard, with real love, we trust. Then, because of this trust, a solution opens up, and life becomes easy. Things start to work out in our life miraculously. We become so relaxed and happy. Unconditional love is a miracle.

Pressuring ourselves to be compassionate and suffering through this pressure is not really compassion. Compassion happens when we understand something deeply and it becomes part of us. Then compassion manifests itself naturally and easily, with no effort. Understanding this, we don't pressure ourselves. This is compassion for the self.

When we love someone unconditionally, it means we don't expect them to love us back. They can push our love away, and we won't mind. We see that this person is unfortunate and needs more love. It doesn't mean that if you give them love, they'll become loving right away. It is more like a drop in a bucket. It doesn't fill the bucket, but it certainly adds to it. Life happens gradually. By giving love to others, we gradually make a difference. And that is what Existence wants—that we make a difference gradually. We get so much joy and blessings by giving love. We recognize that someone doesn't have love, and we give them love without expecting anything from them. This is unconditional love. This is real love. It is not dependent upon any condition. If we say, "Okay, if they accept my love, I will give them love," this is not real love. Having real love makes us happy and joyful. If we have conditional love, our happiness is dependent on the other. If they accept my love, I am happy; if they don't, I am miserable. If we don't have any love, we are miserable all the time. The amount of happiness we have comes from the amount of love we have.

Ego is what we have learned, starting with our first breath, about life. Unfortunately, most of these teachings don't come from love. They come from fear, hatred, and hardship, so they come with very heavy, negative energy. We carry this heavy, negative energy for years in the form of our beliefs or what we have learned. We call these beliefs conditionings. This is what we call ego.

    The best remedy for the ego is to see it or become aware of it. When you see it, it loses its power. Every time you see your ego, it loses more power. When you become aware of the ego enough, it cannot operate anymore. Expressing our feelings, or basically expressing ourselves, helps to expedite our freedom from the ego. By being aware and expressing, we allow the energy of the soul to enter our mind and body. With this energy, we gain the power to overrule our lower self, or ego. Instead, we operate from our higher self, which is divine.

It's not that we don't let the ego take over as mystics. We actually let the ego take over. We let it come out and look at it when it does, so we can become aware of it. As we see it more and more, it becomes less and less. We cannot stop the ego from taking over. It takes over without our permission. Know that the ego is all over us like a cheap suit! The only thing we need to do is to see it and handle it well.

When the worst part of us comes out, it is the best opportunity for us to look at ourselves. It is a golden opportunity to get to know ourselves.

First, we have to see what our problem is. Then we will start noticing how Existence creates situations for us to help us look at our problems.

Everyone is suffering because, if we live a life of materialism, we feel bad. Deep down, we think, "This is not the way. I should be more religious." But if we go towards religion, again we are in conflict because the world values materialism. So we suffer. Everybody lives with this conflict. This struggle has been given to us so that one day we can become totally free of this world.

When cleaning our karma, we often go through hardship. Without hardship, it is difficult to clean karma. Making karma is much easier, but cleaning it is hard. When others are bothering us, especially unjustly, it's because Existence is helping us to clean our karma through them. They are basically helping us.

When others mistreat us, there are two possibilities. One is that we are innocent and they are being unjust. In this situation, the person who has mistreated us will punish themselves eventually. The second possibility is that we really are at fault and the mistreatment from others is an opportunity for us to see our ego, and hopefully what we did won't happen again. If we see and understand what we are doing in the moment, we can stop it. If we don't see it, the negativity inside of us accumulates, and we become heavy. We call this accumulation karma. Someday, we will finally have to learn this lesson, so we can go beyond this limitation.

Sometimes we have to feel bad because if we never felt bad, we would never want to dig deeper into ourselves. Without hardship, we won't worry about finding out why this misery is happening. We won't bother with how our ego is limiting us and reducing our capacity for true joy. We will move through life on autopilot without ever experiencing the limitless joy for which we were meant. Everything is given to us by Existence, even hardship, so we can get to our center, to the joy already living inside of us, waiting to be rediscovered. Every bad feeling is given to us for many good reasons. One is to find out who we are. By finding out who we are, we expand the horizons of our consciousness. This is what growth is.

When we are in a rush or focused on doing something, if someone distracts us, we get upset with them. If we are not in a rush or focusing, we have more freedom and can give space to the other.

When we have a deeper understanding about any inner phenomenon—any issue or limitation, fear or negativity—we become totally free. This is the most important thing in life. This is the meaning of life, freedom from negativities. Freedom means letting go of all that limits us. This freedom is the meaning of life.

Courage, or to be courageous, is one of the more important qualities in both life and mysticism. Courageous people become innovators and pioneers. A courageous person is a strong person. So courage gives strength, and inner strength is always a good thing. If we do something wisely, courage is already part of that doing. Wisdom is both courageous and creates courage too. When we trust, we are wise. Trust basically means trusting Existence. Trusting that everything that happens or will happen has a higher intelligence in it. That intelligence is Existence. We are like a wave that is made up of the same water as the ocean. When the wave trusts the ocean, it is a good thing. If the wave doesn't trust the ocean, imagine the hardship for the wave. Each drop of the ocean has all the flavors of the entire ocean. That means each drop has free will. So we are free to trust the ocean or not. Not trusting creates fear and suffering. Trusting creates inner peace. When we don't trust the ocean because of fear, we cannot be courageous. We worry and doubt everything. But if we are wise, we trust deeply. We are courageous, and a lot of fresh understanding and creativity comes to us.

When we want to do something but can't, it's because somewhere in our childhood we have gotten the impression that this specific thing is not good. There is something negative about this work or activity in our subconscious. Our conscious mind is only three to seven percent of our total consciousness. So when we want something but it's hard for us, the difficulty is coming from the bigger part of us, the unconscious, that doesn't agree with what we want. Our subconscious tells us this is hard, I can't do it, it's beneath me,... We might still continue with the activity and complete it with a lot of hardship, but if we do succeed, it is because the hardship takes us to the deeper parts of our being, where our conscious mind joins with the unconscious, and our wanting becomes total. It comes from our whole being, so we succeed. If our subconscious agrees with us from the start, then completing the task is easy, because the three percent and ninety-seven percent work together.

When we want something deeply, it means that more of our being wants that thing. When we are total, when one hundred percent of our being wants this thing, we are aligned with Existence. We are one with Existence. So when we want something deeply, it just means that we are coming more in line with the will of Existence.

Experiences of past lifetimes sit in our subconscious and become our roots. A tree can never go against its own roots. It's the same with us; we cannot go against our roots. If we do, we destroy ourselves. So we have to do what comes easily or more naturally for us, because if it is easy, it shows that our subconscious or our roots are agreeing with us.

There is a positive side to everything, even something negative like comparison. Everything in Existence has been created to help us grow. When we compare ourselves with others, we lose ourselves. We become confused about who we are. But that is a blessing because this confusion is helping us to find our real self—to find who we really are. Everything in Existence is there to help us grow, even comparison.

The ego wants to be the best in everything, so when it sees that someone is better, it immediately goes to comparison, becomes miserable, and wants to compete. It becomes disappointed in us and says things like, "I expect more of myself; I should be better, more creative, more poetic, more let go,…" We call this phenomenon an inferiority complex. It makes us feel not good enough. So we really better watch our inferiority complex. It is a big step in our growth, if we can see it.

There is a technique that can help us feel better in almost any situation. The technique is to imagine that something worse could have happened. In this way, we see that the situation we are in is not that bad, and we can feel better immediately.

If you want to lose your center, the best way to do so is to compare yourself to someone else. You will immediately fall apart.

Comparing ourselves to others means we want to do what they do, but we want to do it better. We compare ourselves to someone who is like us. As soon as we compare, we want to compete. Competition basically means that one feels they are not good enough the way they are, and they need to become like this other person to have value or importance. Competition is very destructive. It is against Existence. It is against the present moment. If competition becomes a habit, we can't be in the moment anymore. We never enjoy.

Whatever comes from our soul is from the moment. Each moment is extremely fresh and has so much let-go and beauty in it. On the other hand, the mind comes from society and the past. That is why, if we go with our mind, we become miserable. The mind is in conflict with our soul. The past is in conflict with the moment. All our worrying and dissatisfaction come from this conflict. Perfectionism comes from the mind. Real perfection comes when we are in the moment. But perfection, in the eyes of society, tells us we need to do more, have more money, and do better. It is very interesting that, because the mind worries about all these goals, it doesn't give space for them to happen. It prevents them from happening by worrying. The mind makes things harder for us. It tells us these things are hard to do or get. But the fact is that everything is here right now. Society makes us run after things by telling us they are far away. It creates a goal and makes us miserable. Then life becomes a huge struggle, full of arguments, worry, and problems. Our life doesn't work. If we refuse the moment, we can never get anywhere.

If we try not to be in the past, we are already in the past. Why? Because trying comes from the experiences, practices, and know-hows of the past.

The more we meditate or the more we feel love, the more our soul awakens; then, understandings of our soul enter our minds easily. When we feel love, because love brings us to the here and now, it acts like a natural meditation. Meditation basically means gaining the patience needed to stay in the moment. Love automatically gives us patience and the moment. How can you feel impatient with someone for whom you are feeling deep love? It is impossible. When you are angry with someone, you are impatient with them, but the next moment, you can start loving them again and become extremely patient with them.

The higher we go in our inner journey, the less predictable everything becomes. At the beginning, everything is predictable and solid, but the more we grow, the more things become fluid and unpredictable. What we learn from society and our parents comes from thousands of years ago, but Existence changes all the time. It becomes more and more subtle, so what we know is quite outdated.

Whenever society enters, we close ourselves. That is why, if we come into contact with another person, we tend to close ourselves.

The mind goes to the past and brings in the insecurities of the past. These insecurities impact us and cause us to act in ways that might be inappropriate or wrong for what is happening. This bothers people. Then, we get a harsh response from them. This harshness is good because it helps us pay attention to our insecurities and grow from them.

The past obstructs our present perception. It covers the here and now. When we look at any situation through the past, we see only the past and not the now. When this happens, reality doesn't show itself as it is. It is tainted by the shadow of our past experiences. This is what it means to be in the past. We don't see what *is*. We just see what *was* a long time ago, and we project that onto the here and now.

Projecting the past onto the now is heavy. The reason the past has stayed in our subconscious is *because* it was heavy. This heavy stuff stays with us so we can work on it later, and that is a blessing. It comes up again and again, so we can understand it and let it go. Deeper understanding allows us to let go of the heaviness of the past.

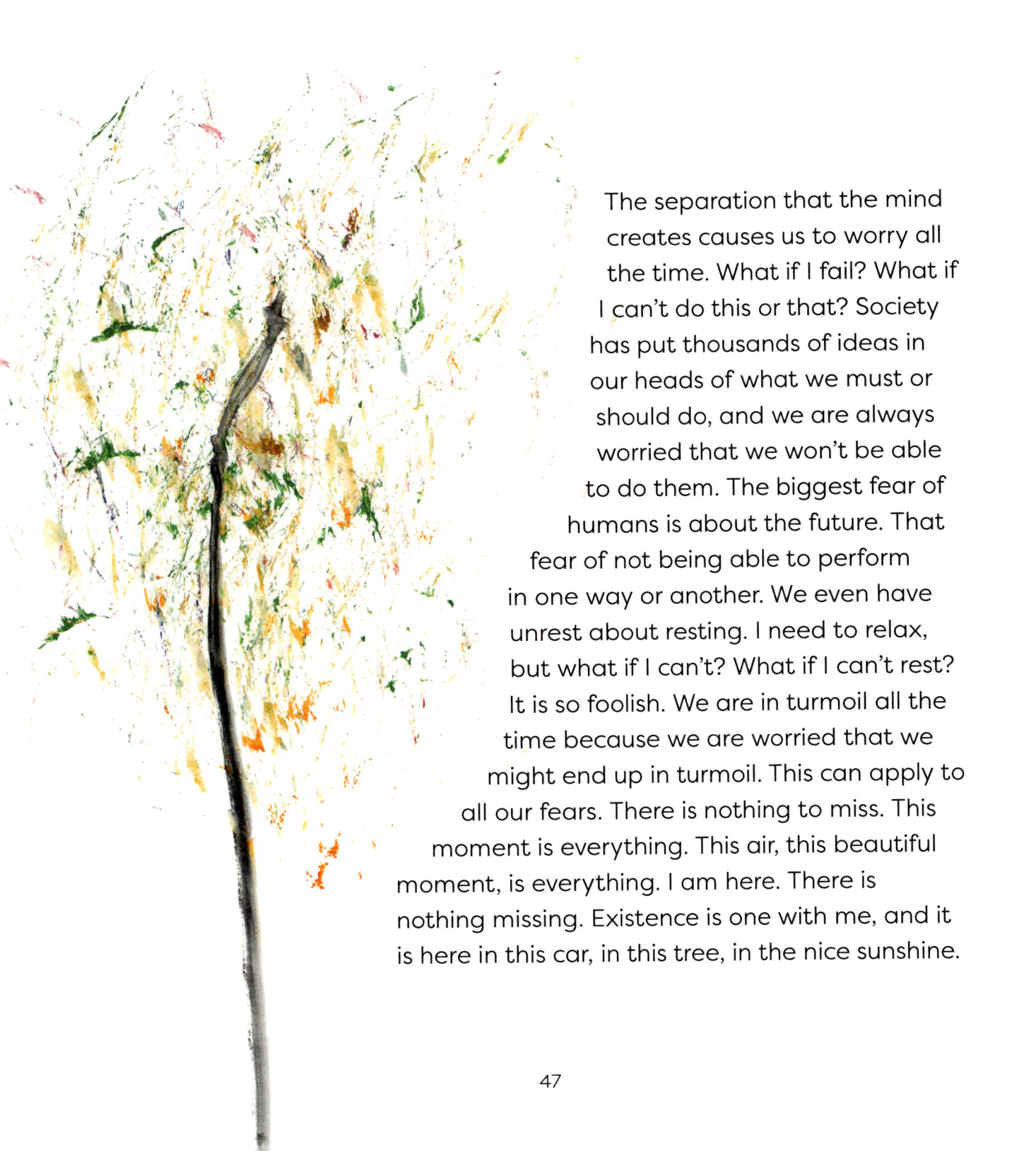

The separation that the mind creates causes us to worry all the time. What if I fail? What if I can't do this or that? Society has put thousands of ideas in our heads of what we must or should do, and we are always worried that we won't be able to do them. The biggest fear of humans is about the future. That fear of not being able to perform in one way or another. We even have unrest about resting. I need to relax, but what if I can't? What if I can't rest? It is so foolish. We are in turmoil all the time because we are worried that we might end up in turmoil. This can apply to all our fears. There is nothing to miss. This moment is everything. This air, this beautiful moment, is everything. I am here. There is nothing missing. Existence is one with me, and it is here in this car, in this tree, in the nice sunshine.

When we are unaware, the mind goes to the past and looks for something negative. When it finds it, we become upset. We have to be aware of our minds. Paying attention to the mind makes us free from the mind.

Whatever helps us grow is called creativity. Only when we experience the here and now are we creative. So if we paint but don't experience the here and now, there will be no growth or creativity in it. Here and now means something new. If I make a painting just like another painting, or even better, it has no value because it does not help me grow. It has no newness or creativity in it. But if something very new comes out of us, it has come from Existence. So painting by itself is not creativity. Only the experience of Existence can help us grow and bring newness to us.

Humans have two possibilities: one is to follow the path of society, which means living our lives according to what we have learned from our relatives, friends, teachers, the kids we knew in kindergarten, middle school, high school, and college, or what we see in magazines and on TV.... Or we can follow the path of God. There is no other alternative. Wherever we go, we are in the energy of others. Even when we are alone, the memories of our past—of friends, family, teachers, and so on—surface. The only way for humans to be free is to join with Existence, which is beyond this earth. If we stay on the path of the society, we will get bothered a lot.

When we are working on our tensions, it helps if there is tension outside of us, because the more we grow, meditate, and understand, the more we get to see that these outside tensions don't affect us as much. Also, outer tensions make us more aware by bothering us, so we want to do something about them. They make us more mature. We see that Existence gives us exactly what we need according to our level of maturity. Something happens and ten people have ten different interpretations of it depending upon which chakra they are in. This is how Existence works with people to help them grow. Existence is so loving. Really, we are one with Existence and there is a higher order in Existence, and therefore us.

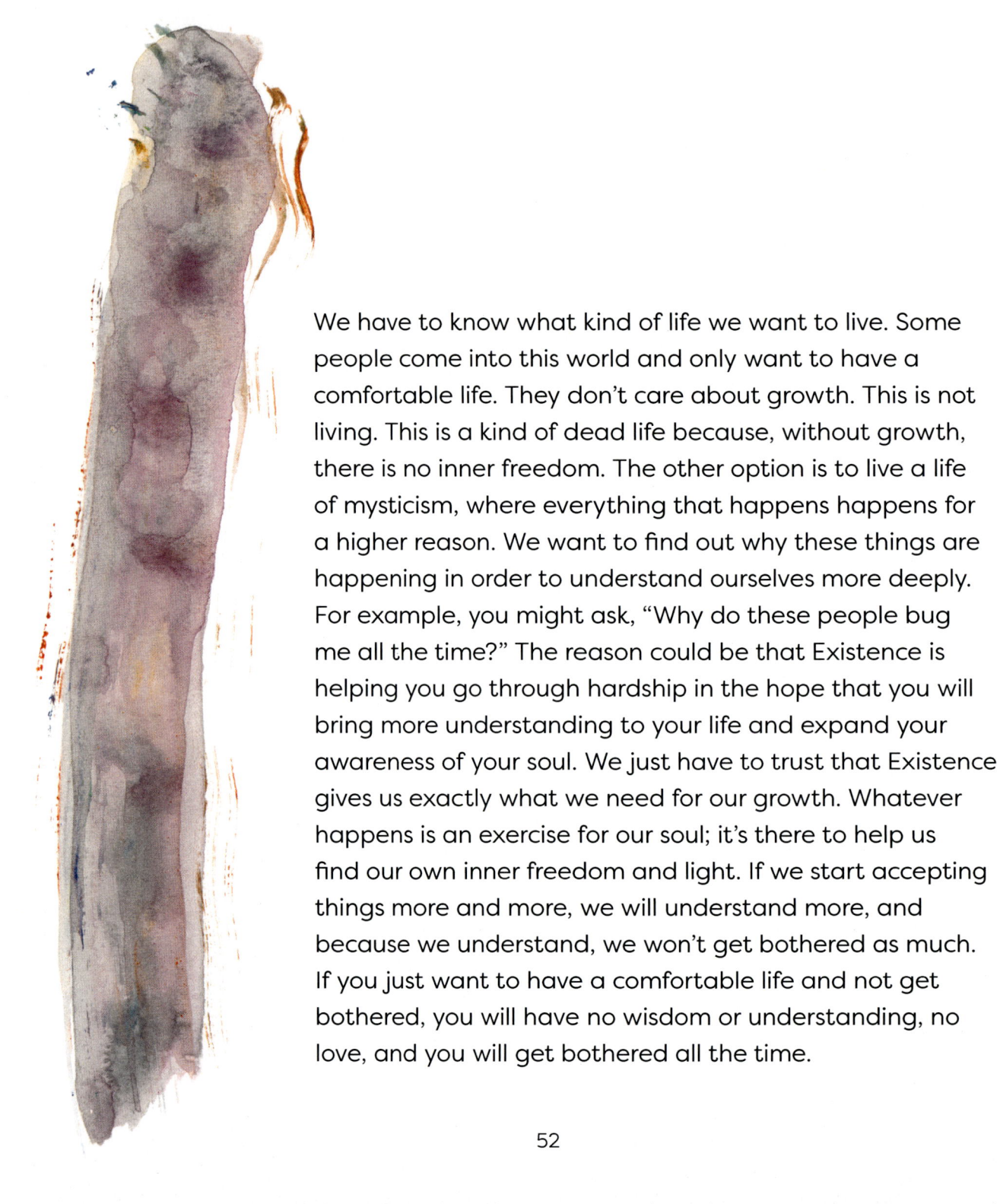

We have to know what kind of life we want to live. Some people come into this world and only want to have a comfortable life. They don't care about growth. This is not living. This is a kind of dead life because, without growth, there is no inner freedom. The other option is to live a life of mysticism, where everything that happens happens for a higher reason. We want to find out why these things are happening in order to understand ourselves more deeply. For example, you might ask, "Why do these people bug me all the time?" The reason could be that Existence is helping you go through hardship in the hope that you will bring more understanding to your life and expand your awareness of your soul. We just have to trust that Existence gives us exactly what we need for our growth. Whatever happens is an exercise for our soul; it's there to help us find our own inner freedom and light. If we start accepting things more and more, we will understand more, and because we understand, we won't get bothered as much. If you just want to have a comfortable life and not get bothered, you will have no wisdom or understanding, no love, and you will get bothered all the time.

Tension mostly comes from resisting or disliking, not approving or hating. Repression means holding anger and irritation inside and not expressing it. This tension gets collected in different parts of our body: in the muscles, the face, the mind, our emotions, in different subtle bodies, even in our toes.

    There is a revolutionary point in our life when we let go of our inner tension. Before this point, any little thing can bother us. We stress over things like, "Why are people late? Why is it so windy? Why do I have a pimple? Why did I say that?" Our inner tension finds all kinds of avenues to make its way to the surface, which is good because the only way to let go of inner tension is to become aware of it. One of the easiest ways to do this is to see how tension plays out in our outer world. When inner tension is gone, everything becomes easy in life because we are relaxed and happy. The mind also has its own workings and tensions; by becoming aware of them, they subside immediately. But usually, when we have inner tension, it doesn't leave us because we are not aware of it. The tension is unconscious, so we suffer unconsciously. When we do become aware of it, we throw the tension out. We can help this process by taking a deep breath and exhaling strongly. It is like when you become conscious of holding the muscles of your leg, you immediately let go of them. You don't hold them tight anymore.

When we carry tension, we need an avenue to regularly release that tension. For example, opening ourselves (expressing) or experiencing deep love opens the heart, and tension is reduced. Meditation can also do this. Otherwise, with tension, we can become sick. Also, the people around us will feel the tension we carry and become bothered too.

Worrying basically means some negativity is boiling up and surfacing from the subconscious. When it does, we feel it, and it becomes worrying. Worrying is attached to our conditioning. It is cultural. It uses conditioning and cultural beliefs and values to determine if something is okay or not. If not okay, we worry. Some picture, scene, or situation can trigger memories from the past in the subconscious, and we become worried *now* for no reason at all. Even something someone says can trigger this phenomenon. Some people who are more intuitive and sensitive can even get a sense of the future and worry about it.

When we are worried, the "I" comes in. This creates separation from the whole, from Existence. We worry that we might not be able to do this or that, but there is nothing to be done. Everything is in this moment. That's all there is. And tomorrow, again, will be this moment. There is only this moment. We really are blessed. We exist. We are Existence. Let's once and for all not separate ourselves from Existence, and see how we feel. We will feel so much freedom. And then, at one point, we will see that we are freedom. Existence is freedom. When we get to this point, our mind also becomes free. It moves without fear or limitation. It never says, "I am afraid I won't get there!" The mind will not be afraid of anything if it is free. The mind exists as we exist. If we separate ourselves, we become small and worried. Our mind becomes limited and afraid. If we live in the moment and become one with Existence, our mind becomes so free and unburdened that our possibilities are limitless!

Worrying happens when the mind goes to the future with doubt or fear. The past is dead, but it is also safe. I can repeat the past and feel safe, but it's dead. The future is alive, but, in the moment, it doesn't exist. This moment is also alive, but we miss what is alive if we approach it from our dead past. If we stay in the moment, we are as free as the wind. It is our mind that creates trouble because it lives in memories of the past. If we are total in this moment and in whatever we do, the mind steps aside, and we become free like the wind.

When we think of something negative, for example, if we are worried for someone, we automatically become tense. Or we might be worried because we said something that, we think, hurt someone. Whatever the reason, worry creates tension in us. If we believe the negativity was our fault, worry includes guilt. We think that I should or shouldn't have done something, or that I should have done something differently. To worry means something might go wrong in the future. Guilt relates to the past. All of these kinds of thoughts create tension. We just have to pay attention to our thoughts. We cannot change how we think, but paying attention to our thoughts makes us more conscious. Consciousness means bringing our soul in, and the soul has the wisdom to understand. Understanding makes it clear that the future will take care of itself, or we will have the ability to take care of it, when the future comes. We will cross that bridge when we come to it.

When we feel pressured by one thing, usually, we can handle it. But when we feel pressured by multiple things, at some point they become too much, and then a seemingly tiny thing can push us over the edge, and we fall apart.

Miracles happen to people who have inner peace. If our inner tensions go away and get replaced by inner peace and calmness, miracles happen. Pressure, hardships, and getting bothered are for people with tension. Where does this tension come from? Since we were born, we have been told, "Do this. Don't do that. Be careful. Look what you did. Make sure you are on time!" They give us so much tension. All this tension becomes our roots, forming the basis of our whole lives. If our roots are based in tension, what kind of life can we have? We are condemned to a life full of fear and tension.

    We can look at tension from different aspects. All layers of our lives have memory systems where tension can be stored. The brain has memory cells, but the body also has memory. For example, if we get into an accident and the body gets hurt, it will keep that memory and hold tension around that area until we let go of it, which is an art in itself. Or if we get a toothache, the tension we hold around the pain of the tooth stays with us a long time after the pain is gone. It does so as both a memory and as the tension we created in the body around that pain.

When we are enjoying and our heart is open, we don't create tension. An open heart reduces tension; a closed heart creates tension. The heart closes when the mind comes in, bringing fear, negativity, or judgment to a situation. Worry and tension make us age faster and become sick. Almost all physical and emotional problems are caused by tension, and tension happens because we have so many negative thoughts that make us worry. We need to pay attention to our thoughts and see their negativity for what it is: just the mind doing its job. When we see this, the mind loses its power over us, and we turn to positivity.

Anyone who doesn't want to look at themselves blames others. Also, when we are nervous, we blame others. If we don't have tension, we don't blame ourselves or anyone else. When we don't have tension, we don't see anything wrong. When we have tension, we see many things as wrong, and it's always somebody else's fault. How can we not be tense? By deeply and sincerely understanding others and ourselves, we relax, and this leads to pure love. When we feel love, we are not under pressure anymore, and therefore, we are not tense. We are open. Other people trust us; we trust others, and life becomes sweet.

We cannot trust people who cannot acknowledge their weaknesses, but if someone is open to acknowledging their weaknesses, we trust them. If we feel that people don't trust us, we have to look at ourselves and see if maybe we don't want to see our own weaknesses. If we are not open to hearing about and understanding our own weaknesses, we fight back. This is a life-transforming lesson. It can change our life, if we can pay attention to it.

When we do not accept others, they suffer, and we also suffer. We suffer because we want them to be different. We don't like the way they are. So every time they do something we don't like, it gets on our nerves. This is what we call suffering. When we say no to ourselves, we suffer twice as much. How do we say no to ourselves? By being negative about ourselves. By denying ourselves. We might say, "I can't do it. This is too hard." Or we may say, "I know if I go there, everything will be horrible." We brainwash ourselves with negative thoughts, but if we get there and nothing is wrong, then we are okay again. We see that we worried for nothing. This negativity is saying no to the self. It is very important to see this and become aware of how we suffer when we say no.

When someone disapproves of us or dislikes something we've done, we get upset. This is just the nature of being human. Even a spiritual person gets upset when someone is not happy with them. But when *we* get upset, we suffer. When a spiritual person gets upset, they don't suffer because they don't let the upset go deeper into them. It is totally normal to get upset or uncomfortable when someone disapproves of us. How we handle this discomfort is the important thing. When we encounter someone who is upset with us, we just need to accept that this person is upset with me, and I don't like it, and that's fine. It is as natural as breathing. We don't become miserable when we are breathing. By accepting, we transform, because acceptance transforms things. We can be upset, but we don't have to be miserable. Acceptance is a transforming force.

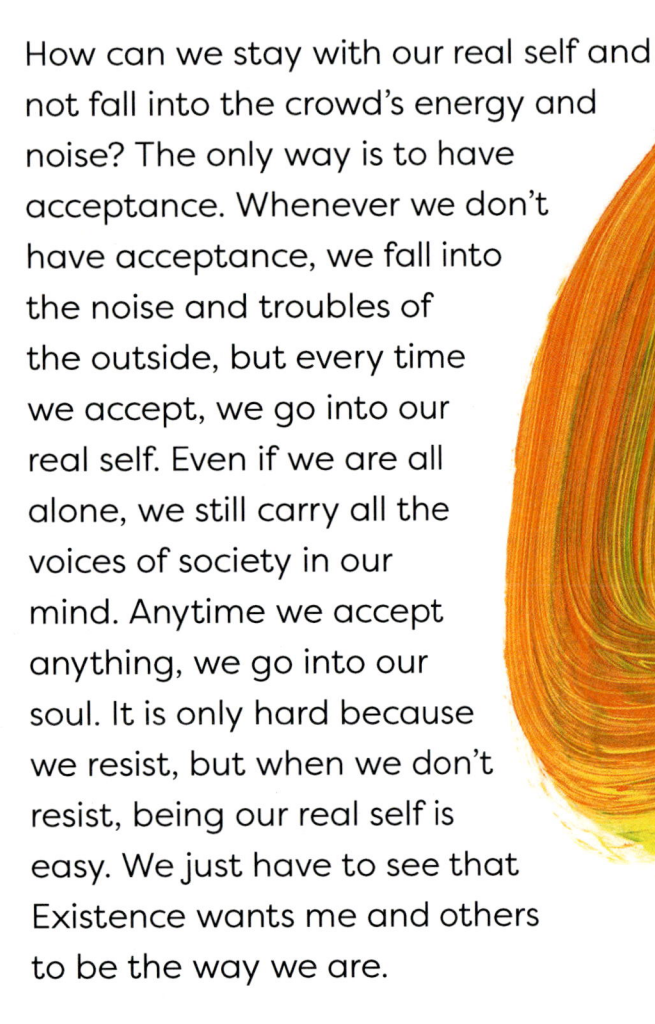

How can we stay with our real self and not fall into the crowd's energy and noise? The only way is to have acceptance. Whenever we don't have acceptance, we fall into the noise and troubles of the outside, but every time we accept, we go into our real self. Even if we are all alone, we still carry all the voices of society in our mind. Anytime we accept anything, we go into our soul. It is only hard because we resist, but when we don't resist, being our real self is easy. We just have to see that Existence wants me and others to be the way we are.

Being stupid or seeing someone we think is stupid can become very frustrating because we think being stupid is bad. But when we become mature, we see that stupid is so advanced. Everything that is is God. The space of God has everything in it—stupid and non-stupid, intelligent and non-intelligent. Since everything is God, everything is advanced. The moment we realize this, we never become frustrated with anything ever again. We love it if we are or anyone else is stupid. We laugh, and life is so fun. We see that it is a blessing to be stupid, and it is also a blessing not to be stupid. Just the fact that we are alive is such a blessing.

In nature, there is no perfection. When we look at nature, we see that everything is unique. An artificially symmetric tree or bush is so ugly. The beauty of a tree is in its imperfections. Perfection makes things ugly because there is no room for improvement or growth. It is almost like being dead. Beauty comes from improvement and growth. Nature is not supposed to be perfect. We have invented perfectionism, and it's hurting us. Our entire life is affected by it, and it creates great suffering. If we let go of our perfectionism, our life becomes beautiful. Our life becomes perfect.

What is perfectionism? It means that, when our room isn't clean, for example, we suffer because of it. Why? Because now the room is not perfect. If we just accept things, we don't suffer. We enter our messy room, and it doesn't bother us. We go on doing our things. This is having acceptance. This person is not a perfectionist. He accepts his room and is happy. We have so many things that we think are wrong with us, and we suffer all the time because of them. This suffering takes our energy constantly. This is why so many people are addicted to sugar, coffee, or food, because they need something to replace their lost energy. And so many diseases come from this overeating and tension. We don't have acceptance for ourselves, others, or situations, and because of this, we are constantly in turmoil. A perfectionist finds problems in everything. So it makes sense to understand that perfection is not healthy for us.

But nothing is perfect on planet Earth because it is a dual world. When two become one, this is perfection, there is light. Look at electricity. Two opposite energies meet in a light bulb, and there is light. Humans are also two in terms of energy. There is negative and positive energy in all of us. We call these energies male and female. When these two meet and become one, we also have inner light. We call this light enlightenment. We can call this perfection.

The mind is not capable of understanding the inner world. But sometimes when we don't understand, it just means that we are preparing ourselves for future understanding. They go hand in hand.

This is a dual planet. Because of this, two kinds of people exist on Earth: those more focused on the mind and those who live from the heart. The heart is female, the mind is male. There is a third kind that is very rare, and that is people who have both qualities—heart and mind. If a person balances these two, they become enlightened. They become a Buddha. A balance between the heart and mind is needed. Then, the third kind of human is created.

Love means acceptance. Someone who doesn't accept doesn't have love. Someone who has acceptance doesn't get frustrated easily. Anything we don't accept is something we need to work on so we can become free of rejection— so that our rejection can turn to acceptance and love. The path of the female is the path of love, which means the path of acceptance. The path of the male is to meditate and bring witnessing, because the male alone cannot bring love. This is very subtle. Through meditation, the male will eventually get to love, and through love, the female will eventually get to awareness and witnessing. On Earth, there are two poles: the female and the male. The beauty of this Existence is that these two poles exist, and for each pole there is a special path for growth—love and meditation.

As we know, there is male and female energy in every person. Problems arise because our male and female are separated. The female doesn't like the harshness of the male, so when the male is harsh, the female withdraws. The male becomes angry without the gentleness of the female. But if our male becomes gentle, our female energy stays with him, and we become centered. The male can become gentle if he becomes more aware. We have to see what is happening inside of us and become aware of the interactions between our male and female energies. Then we become totally free. When the male becomes open and inviting, the female joins with him. We become whole. With this wholeness comes abundance, love, vastness, miracles, happiness, ecstasy, and more. They all come to us. The purpose of our existence becomes fulfilled. We become free.

Understanding takes us beyond the two poles of male and female. The female often reacts by getting hurt, while the male becomes aggressive, pushing everyone around and creating trouble. We have to go beyond these two poles so we don't feel bad anymore. The only way to go beyond these two is with understanding. When we understand, we become free. Every time we understand, our soul expands. Eventually, it gets to a point where the soul has expanded so much that, all of a sudden, it sparks and shines a light on our whole consciousness. We become enlightened.

So why do we get bothered? Because this is our way to growth. When we get bothered, we have to find a deeper understanding to get out of our unhappiness. When we do, our awareness of our soul expands. It is like a tension-relaxation technique for our soul. Every time we become free, our consciousness expands until, one day, it becomes totally free and we become enlightened. Even when we become enlightened, we still grow, but in a different dimension. We don't have to suffer anymore.

On planet Earth, there are two opposite energies that create life. One is softer, the other is harder or harsher. Every person has to have these two energies within them in order to be alive. Life starts when these two opposite energies interact. Our inner harshness and softness are our intelligence. They are energy from the universe, and each has its own characteristics. These energies can be more refined or less refined. The softness often cannot work with the harshness. Softness gives space to harshness because this is a characteristic of softness, to give space. So when harshness shows up, softness tends to withdraw, but harshness without softness is too rough. We need to have both together, balancing each other.

There is male and female energy in every human being. The female comes from the mother, the male from the father. Some people are more female, and some are more male. To be balanced between the male and female is where we want to be, because then we taste our soul. This is what pure joy is. In reality, though, most of the time we are either more female or more male. The path of the female is the path of acceptance. When we are more female, all we need to do is accept and to remember that everything that happens, happens by the hands of Existence.

    Existence is not our enemy. In fact, Existence is the best friend we have. When we understand this deeply, we trust that *everything* that happens is good, even if it seems bad. We trust that there is a higher and loving reason for everything that happens. This is the reason for the saying, "God works in mysterious ways." So acceptance is a path for the female. Actually, this is the path for everyone. Anybody who accepts life becomes joyful. We accept because God is running the show. We don't need to worry, and not worrying at all means enjoyment.

Female is always where she should be. She is relaxed and vast. Male runs all the time. It can never relax.

We protect ourselves all the time. We have two opposite energies within us that we call male and female. Both of them are always on the edge, ready to get hurt. When the female gets hurt, she protects herself by withdrawing. When the male gets hurt, he becomes aggressive. Beyond the inner male and female is the divine. It doesn't get involved with withdrawal or aggression. It doesn't need to protect at all. The divine is very strong, like the male, but also has a refined love, which is a trait of the female. And that is who we are. We are beyond male and female.

Before we reach the divine in ourselves, we are either more female, which makes us more people-oriented, or we are more male, which makes us more task-oriented. If we are still people-oriented or task-oriented, we are lacking some deeper understanding. With deeper understanding, we go beyond duality to the divine. The qualities of the divine are very much those of the strong female without a negative side. The divine is all about love and deep acceptance. We still have the mind because we are on this planet, but we are the divine, also. This is the job of the master: to remind us that we are beyond duality. We are one with Existence. We are pure oneness. We are the strong female. We can go beyond the duality of this planet while we are on this planet. We call this enlightenment.

Anyone who is people-oriented loves to connect with others. They are more open than task-oriented people. Because of this openness, they get hurt easily when they don't feel love from another. Task-oriented people get hurt if the task is not done or if they are not successful in their doings.

When a people-oriented person and a task-oriented person get close to each other, there is softness between them. But if they see someone like themselves, they don't see that person deeply or connect with them because they are too similar. Usually, we don't see ourselves because we don't like what we see. So if we see someone similar to us, we don't like them either. We reject someone who is like us and become attracted to someone who is our opposite. If I am a people-oriented person, I will get along with a task-oriented person, and vice versa. Anytime we get close to someone, difficulties arise, but with similar people, we get into trouble right off the bat. Just socializing with them might be okay, but if we get close, problems arise quickly.

The male feels good when he feels his time has been fruitful and productive, and he has accomplished something. If the male focuses his productivity and drive on his inner growth, he is using his talent in the best way. He uses it to work on himself. The female enjoys when there is no structure and there is relaxation. She takes things lightly; she goes with the flow. That is how she enjoys. If a woman works on herself, it's because her male side is doing it. The female is happy wherever she is, so she doesn't bother to do things. The male makes us do things. Thank God, we have both male and female in us, so we can both rest and work. When the male gets tired, the female comes in, and we rest. When we are tired of resting, the male, who has recharged and is full of energy, is ready to come in and get to work.

A woman is sensitive. If something goes wrong in her life, she withdraws. Withdrawing means she either becomes angry or pouts and becomes sad. A divorce can do that. Some people stay withdrawn for the rest of their lives after a divorce. And if they get into a new relationship with that withdrawn feeling, the new relationship won't work either. Once you withdraw, it stays with you forever, unless you look at it deeply, understand it, and clean it. Healing needs deep understanding and love. It takes a lot of work to heal. Most people become bitter, and their mind is always negative. We need to go beyond the mind, but to get beyond the mind, first we have to go to the positive. In the positive, we can let go of the negative. When we deeply understand, we go beyond the mind. We get to absolute love, absolute freedom, and absolute let go.

The mind is, or our thoughts are, always in the past. The mind cannot experience the moment unless it turns it into the past. Then it can associate with it. Also, the mind mostly remembers the negativities of the past. Someone who is in the mind a lot, then, is always in the past. Women are mostly in the emotional body. The emotional body cannot go to the past. It is always in the moment. But how does one get to the emotional body? First, the mind comes in and, using our conditionings from the past, determines whether what is happening is negative. If so, the female falls into the emotional body. This is her way of rebelling against what is happening. She goes to the second chakra, the emotional body, to rebel. So her male side filters what is happening through the mind and then hands it over to the emotional body.

Our inner male listens to or obeys the voice of society, so it doesn't like whatever society doesn't approve of. We have to look and see what the truth is, not just what society approves or disapproves of. The male (and society) usually doesn't like softness. It doesn't like crying and weakness, or withdrawing and passivity, because it doesn't understand them. The male always wants power. It doesn't understand the language of let-go. We need to look at things with deeper understanding, not just from the point of view of society. When we do this, we become happy.

Where do feelings and thoughts come from? Our female side basically contains all our feelings. Male on the other hand, is all our memories, and memories can turn into thoughts. When the female is bothered, she brings in negative feelings. The female or male alone don't have the tools to understand. It is only when these two opposite poles (male and female) balance each other or come together and become united that understanding happens, and when understanding happens, the female brings in all the positive emotions.

What is an emotional wound? In the mind, there are negative memories, and if some event triggers these memories, they pop up to the surface, which means they come to the now. Then, the negative energy these memories carry goes to the second chakra. From the second chakra, there is a direct pathway to the emotional body. The negative energy from the memories enters the emotional body and stirs up different negative emotions. We call this whole process having emotional wounds.

The female inside both genders has been repressed for ages. She has not been allowed to express herself. So when we are more female, it's hard for us to express ourselves. Because we can't express, we become more passive. We need to know that it's not our fault. The fault comes from societal beliefs. It is hard in society to express our feelings. Society is more geared toward facts and reasoning. Female energy is more geared toward emotions, art, and love. When we can't express our emotions, we tend to have more emotional breakdowns. But just understanding all this might help us to express more freely.

Awareness means giving space to the female within us. She feels comfortable with this support, and she shines. She participates with our inner male, and we feel joy, happiness, and fun. Fun happens when the male and female meet within us. Just paying attention to our inner energies creates an environment of enjoyment and softness.

When we are born, we are very innocent, open, fragile, and pure. But the world is harsh. It pushes us until, gradually, we learn to defend ourselves. When we defend, it is more like a fight, which creates wounds inside of us. These wounds stay with us until we get to the age when we have to start dealing with them more maturely, with understanding and looking deeper. This is where mysticism comes in to help us.

We exist; therefore, we are a part of Existence. Existence is whatever exists, but because we have been given a name, we feel separate from Existence. Our name has utilitarian benefits, but unfortunately, it prevents our joy, because to be joyful means to put the "I," the barrier between us and our soul, aside. Our name reinforces this idea of "me" as separate from you, so, in many ways, being given a name has hurt us. It makes us believe that we are separate from everything and everyone. But the fact is, we are all one.

When we make more and more money, we start thinking that people want us only for our money. If anyone gets close to us, we think it is only for our money and not for who we are. Then we begin to feel worthless. The more money we have, the more worthless we feel. It is amazing how more money can make us feel small and not good enough. When we have less money, we feel people like us for ourselves, and that makes us happy. We think money will bring us eternal happiness, so we always want more of it, but if we look deeper, we see that is not the case. Money comes with a lot of baggage. It comes with fear, sadness, depression, and separation. When we have money, we fear losing it too.

The person who is afraid escapes from growing.

Why are we so attached to our false views of the self? Views like, "I'm so great. I am so good. I never make mistakes?" It is because, from childhood, if we did anything wrong, people (teachers, parents, friends, siblings, etc.) scolded us. Now we feel ashamed when we think we've done something wrong. There's so much pressure to be the best, and because of this, tension piles up in us. God forbid, we make a mistake. There is so much fear of doing the wrong thing that we have to pretend that we are good. Even as adults, when we break a dish, part of us wants to hide the dish for fear of being scolded. When these types of activities continue, where we feel we have to hide our mistakes, we start to believe falsely about ourselves. We believe we are not good, or not good enough. Then, in every situation in the future, we carry this image with us—in our marriage, at work, and while socializing. We always feel less than. What a waste. What silly suffering this is!

Negativity is a waste of time.

If we have some kind of chronic physical problem, it is because we have fear in our subconscious. Otherwise, we will only get sick every once in a while for a specific reason, like eating bad food. Fear creates a certain negative frequency that destroys different parts of the body over time.

The problem with the mind is that it blows things out of proportion. It has a tendency to exaggerate everything. We kill an ant and say we shot an elephant. This is how we make ourselves important. The mind also creates scenarios and condemns us. For example, you are cranky one day, which is very natural, and the mind comes in and says, "You are so mean all the time!" We either think we are bad or we think we are the best thing on the planet! These two extremes are there because of exaggeration. We have to watch our mind and see the subtlety of the tricks it plays. When you are cranky, see that it is temporary and not something that defines you. If you are nice, see that it also comes and goes. Believing in the extremes the mind creates is unhealthy. They give us a false image of who we are, and then we live out of that false image for the rest of our lives. We have to pay attention to the tricks the mind uses against us.

There is a law of Existence that says anytime we want to defend ourselves, we aren't seeing the truth of what has really happened—we alter what is in a way that helps us defend the self. But defending the self is funny in itself because there is no self, except in our imagination. So the mind goes to something that is not true in order to defend something that is untrue. The mind sees things in a way that defends or favors our point of view, and often in doing so, the mind exaggerates. We exaggerate or say something that is either not true or just half true. Everybody does that when they want to defend.

When we blame others, even if someone agrees with us, inside, they turn against us. If we blame others all the time, everyone becomes our enemy. People will not like us. We need to understand that fault doesn't exist. Basically, nobody is at fault. Existence does everything, and even though on the surface it might look like things are bad, deep inside whatever happens is good for everyone. If we look deeper, we will see that everything has a divine purpose. When we don't like something, it is because we are looking at it superficially. If we look deeper, we will see that everything is perfect. Existence is happening. Our mind has been programmed by society, and most of this programming is against the flow of Existence. This programming originated thousands of years ago, but people are still going along with it today. The fact is, there is only Existence. We are Existence. Everyone is Existence.

When you don't use the mind for a while and then start using it again, you feel heavy. But people who use the mind all the time get used to it, so it doesn't become heavy for them. It is a luxury to not use the mind all the time.

When we are passive and we don't like something that someone is doing, if they are someone with whom we are not close, we may stay passive for a long time. At some point, however, we will reach our boiling point, and then passivity turns to aggression. With someone close to us, like a spouse, we simply become aggressive if we don't like something.

When we are upset, it shows there is something we are not accepting. The reason we don't accept is because our upbringing doesn't allow it. Let's look more deeply at this. When we don't accept something, we fall apart because we consider it to be bad. When this happens, we have three choices. We can hold it in, which is repression, or we can lash out, which is expression in a harsh way. We call this aggression. Finally, we can express ourselves in a gentle manner, which we call assertiveness. If we have a deeper understanding, however, we will accept things as they are without the need for any of these three. Life becomes so uncomplicated. Simple is deep.

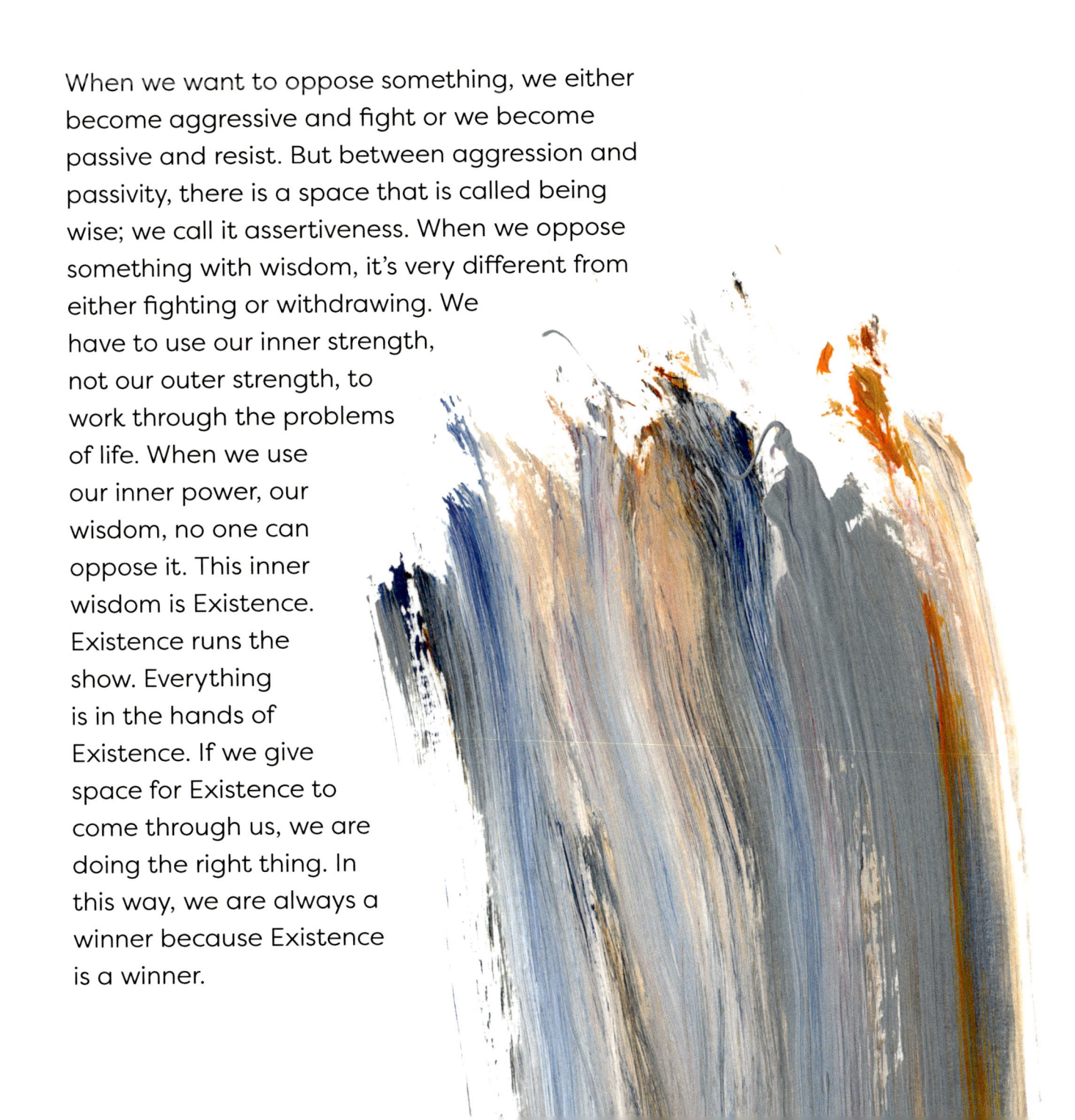

When we want to oppose something, we either become aggressive and fight or we become passive and resist. But between aggression and passivity, there is a space that is called being wise; we call it assertiveness. When we oppose something with wisdom, it's very different from either fighting or withdrawing. We have to use our inner strength, not our outer strength, to work through the problems of life. When we use our inner power, our wisdom, no one can oppose it. This inner wisdom is Existence. Existence runs the show. Everything is in the hands of Existence. If we give space for Existence to come through us, we are doing the right thing. In this way, we are always a winner because Existence is a winner.

Some people are only interested in eating and sleeping. They don't like to do anything. Consequently, their energy accumulates and turns into sadness and bitterness. It turns into negativity.

When we resist, life doesn't work. If we don't resist, anything we do works smoothly and joyfully. Life wants to flow, like energy or blood flows. Resistance disrupts this flow. Resistance opposes life, and then life becomes complicated and full of emotional constipation—full of emotional wounds. There is a magic in not resisting. When we try to hide things or be tricky or want to control or change things, when we worry or are afraid, we are resisting. When we don't do these things, we trust. We don't resist and miracles happen. Life is about miracles, but because everybody is resisting one thing or another, miracles are dead today.

A little bit of resistance is needed for us to be alive. Life is basically made by the opposition of the two energies inside of us—the male and the female. So a little bit of resistance is healthy. It helps us grow and understand.

Let's talk about good and bad in relation to our choices. If we think that a certain outcome is good, then we are happy, and we say this was a good choice. But if we make a choice and later on the results of that choice go against our conditionings or our belief system, we suffer because we think we have done wrong. So a bad choice is really dependent on our point of view or our belief system. But in Existence everything just is. It is not bad or good. And in reality, Existence is in charge of what happens here on Earth, and sometimes "bad" things need to happen for a higher purpose or balance. Existence imparts a higher good or purpose that has no opposite. No bad.

The more aware we become, the more we become aware of our ego. Then it becomes optional for us to go with the ego or not. Most of the time, if we are egoistic, it's because we are not aware of it. We might brag and show off, but we do it because we are unaware. We have been doing this for so long that it has become a habit. Ego is just an old habit. We do it without knowing that we are doing it. The nature of humans is that they want to be good. In general, the only reason we do something negative is because we are not aware of it. It has become a habit.

Becoming aware of the truth is called awareness. With awareness, we see the truth about ourselves instead of having an imaginary view of ourselves. We call this imaginary view of the self the ego. To become aware of the truth about ourselves breaks the ego. Then all thoughts of, "I am so great. I am so wonderful" go out the window. With awareness, we eliminate separation from others and, therefore, the need for pride.

When our awareness grows, we move beyond duality. The less awareness we have, the more we fall into the trap of duality. For example, when our awareness is low and we get close to someone in friendship, we both love them more and hate them more, too. But when our awareness grows, we go beyond friendship. We enter into real love. Real love is beyond duality and only happens to a person who is more aware. Real love happens when we become one with the other, which takes us to oneness with God. In God, there is no hate and no friendship. With God, there is just the purity we call love.

The whole purpose of life is to grow so that we experience higher quality. We are the agents of this growth. It doesn't matter what we do—we resist, we don't resist, we think, we don't think, we fall into our emotions, or we don't—they are all a part of growing higher. This is life doing its thing.

Bringing mysticism into our lives means we commit to working on ourselves intensely. We commit to seeking to know ourselves. But if the ego becomes big, we cannot work on ourselves. We cannot know ourselves. A big ego becomes a hindrance to knowing the self and being aware. So if we commit to working on ourselves, we have to watch for the ego and not let it become big and take over.

Understanding the truth, feeling love, and/or having a peaceful mind allows the energy of God to pour into you—you get filled with God's energy. This is pure joy.

PAINTINGS
by Sharam

VIEW AND PURCHASE GICLÉE PRINTS

VISIT:
Sharam.org

Made in the USA
Columbia, SC
27 June 2023

19512750R00066